T0380928

Heroes of Faith in a Contemporary World

In a

Contemporary

World

Fishers of Men

By Dr. G. Yvette Boatwright

AuthorHouse™
1663 Liberty Drive
Bloomington, IN 47403
www.authorhouse.com
Phone: 833-262-8899

Because of the dynamic nature of the Internet, any web addresses or links contained in this book may have changed
since publication and may no longer be valid. The views expressed in this work are solely those of the author and do not
necessarily reflect the views of the publisher, and the publisher hereby disclaims any responsibility for them.

Any people depicted in stock imagery provided by Getty Images are models,
and such images are being used for illustrative purposes only.
Certain stock imagery © Getty Images.

This book is printed on acid-free paper.

Scripture quotations marked KJV are from the Holy Bible, King James Version (Authorized Version). First published
in 1611. Quoted from the KJV Classic Reference Bible, Copyright © 1983 by The Zondervan Corporation.

ISBN: 978-1-6655-7210-1 (sc)
ISBN: 978-1-6655-7211-8 (e)

Library of Congress Control Number: 2022918087

Print information available on the last page.

Published by AuthorHouse 08/13/2024

authorHOUSE

Table of Contents

Acknowledgements

My deepest appreciation to my Family, my parents, my siblings Kenneth, Runette, Dianne, Debra, Teressa and Jacqueline. To my extended family Katie.

A special thanks to Bishop Leake, whom the Lord directed to encourage me to complete this project.

I owe a debt of gratitude to Jonathan Honesty and Brandon Williams for computer technology support and typing.

To my nephews Robbie Stucks, Deon, Javontae Sims, Dianne and Keyia for the photographs. I am grateful for their selflessly helping, with the completion of this project.

Most important, my sincere gratitude to our Father in Heaven for his indescribable gift; to our Lord Jesus for his grace, truth and love; and to the Holy Spirit for his faithful guidance to this project.

Foreword

"And he gave some, apostles; and some, prophets; and some, evangelists; and some, pastors and teachers; For the perfecting of the saints, for the work of the ministry, for the edifying of the body of Christ…" Ephesians 4:11-12.

In Heroes of Faith in a Contemporary World, Dr. G. Yvette Boatwright captures the very essence of Ephesians 4:11-12. This offering speaks of how the Holy Spirit uses those who are open and obedient to the voice and guidance of the Holy Spirit. She provides a great balance between character and calling. She offers testimonies about how the Lord uses women and men in the work of the ministry.

I am amazed at how the Lord has sent many people in her life who helped to shape, mold, and encourage her in Christian ministry as well as Christian living. This book is about Christian ministry, but also Christian maturity. She reminds us that the complete work of salvation is about walking in the fruit and the gifts of the Holy Spirit. It is evident that the Lord's hand has been upon Dr. Boatwright for a long time!

She has captured the work of the ministry of others who have been on this journey with her, helped her, encouraged her, and corrected her in the way of the Lord. We are encouraged in this writing to continue in the way of the Lord walking in the power of the Holy Spirit.

It is my prayer that you too, will be moved by the rich insights from this book. May you find this offering exciting, encouraging, engaging, informational, informative, interesting, scripturally sound, and solid, as well as spirit-filled!

Bishop Eric Leake, Presiding Bishop
African Methodist Episcopal Zion Church (AMEZ)

Heroes of Faith in a Contemporary World

Introduction

We can walk with God in changing times. Our world has changed dramatically (pre and post pandemic) over the past two years - yet God has not changed. He wants us to stand strong in our faith. Hebrew 11: 1 explains "Now faith is the substance of things hoped for, the evidence of things not seen". We get this faith looking unto Jesus, the author and finisher of our faith (Hebrews 12: 2).

The purpose of this book is to provide keys to getting direction from God. The first step is choosing to walk with him in God's plans and purposes. Walking in agreement with God. Amos 3:3 says "Can two walk together except they be agreed?" The answer is no! Walking in agreement with God requires obedience to His will and moving in his timing.

Heroes of the Faith is written to showcase the lives of contemporary Christians. Each ministry was built by faith and obedience to God's direction. Each hero directs an active soul winning, Kingdom building ministry. Each ministry is faith-based and financially supported by Christian believers.

Heroes of the Faith showcases the testimony of three Christians who championed the keys to walking with God. They completed divine assignments and provided examples to follow. These ministries champion faith for assignments:

Bishop Calvin McNeil - Gethsemane Apostolic Church, Lynchburg, SC.
Reverend Ernestine Black – Pine Grove Progressive Church, Utica, Mississippi.
Doctor G. Y. Boatwright- Jesus Ministries, Chicago, IL.

History of the Ministry

Gethsemane Apostolic Church began with humble beginnings with the late Elder Shem Ellis, approximately 17 adults and 5 children in November of 1979. The saints first assembled under a pecan tree beside an old warehouse. The first services were conducted in an old warehouse called the "Boozer". Under the leadership of

Elder Shem, the church continued to worship in the warehouse for two years and six months. After a brief illness, Elder Ellis passed away in May of 1981.

Our present pastor, Bishop Calvin McNeil, was standing by ready, willing and available. He was anointed, called and sent by God to the Lynchburg area in 1981. At that time, Bishop McNeil wore the title of Elder Calvin McNeill. He, his wife, their two children and a small group of saints continued worshiping in the warehouse for two years and nine months.

After much fasting, praying and seeking God for answers, God blessed the ministry to purchase 12 acres of land on Hwy. 76 in Lynchburg, SC. God allowed the saints to march into our first sanctuary in May of 1984. The Church continues to grow and an expansion was added to the first church in 1991.

Over the years, Gethsemane Apostolic has grown to consist of several members housed in a custom built facility. The church has evolved into an abundantly equipped ministry that now services the congregates and the community through life changing ministries such as: deacons, usher board, missionary department, brotherhood, Women's Department, Youth Department, Sunday School, Audio/Visual Ministry and choirs.

God gave Pastor McNeil a vision for the second phase of the Gethsemane Apostolic, and construction began on a larger sanctuary in 2003. During the erection of the second building, Bishop McNeil and the church family were faced with many obstacles and hardships, but they continued to do the will of God. On June 18th, 2005, the current edifice was dedicated to the Lord. It was a time of rejoicing, praising and thanking God for His numerous blessings. After approximately 8 years under the strong spiritual leadership and financial guidance of Bishop McNeil, the Gethsemane church family conducted a mortgage burning ceremony on June 15, 2013 to celebrate the paying off of our current sanctuary.

Today, Gethsemane continues not to be a building for building sake, but it is deliberately purposed to provide the necessary spaces for God's people to minister effectively and to take the Kingdom message to the nations.

Bishop McNeil

Born in 1947 in Pamplico S.C.
Education – High School Graduate

Bishop McNeil was raised in church. The ministries that he encountered in his early life didn't demonstrate the lifestyle that reflected what Jesus taught in the Bible. Consequently, he didn't consider the Church or Christianity seriously.

Bishop McNeil's Conversion Experience

After completing high school, he obtained employment as a welder. Later, the Lord blessed him to become self-employed by establishing a successful trucking company.

While enjoying and exploring his youthful desires and dreams the Lord began to intervene powerfully in his life and affairs. Totally engulfed in a world of work, regular partying, whiskey drinking, motor-cycle riding and dare-devil activities, Bishop McNeil had a Damascus Road experience.

Bishop McNeil's encounter with Jesus Christ impacted his life-transformation. Suddenly his desires changed and the spirit of the Lord invaded his life. He was 30 years old. Bishop McNeil yielded to the call and began to surrender his life, his will and his possessions to Christ.

Bishop McNeil was converted to Jesus Christ on January 1, 1978, and totally surrendered his life to Christianity. God called him to preach in 1979. God spoke to him in the spirit, his response was "I'll go". He preached his trial sermon. The title was from Isaiah 55:6 "Seek ye the Lord while he may be found. Call ye upon him while he is near."

The Spirit of God confirmed his call to ministry during the service by healing and blessing the congregation.

Bishop McNeil's Teachings

Bishop McNeill teaches the fundamental biblical principles of the Bible from Genesis to Revelations. He teaches that the Bible is the unadulterated, infallible word of God.

Bishop McNeil teaches that the blood of Jesus cleanses us and that the Holy Ghost helps us according to Acts 1:8 "But ye shall receive power after that the Holy Ghost is come upon you".

Bishop believes the scriptures, Jesus taught that a man must be born again, being born of water and the Holy Spirit. He believes that baptizing must be done in the name of Jesus, the Father and the Holy Spirit.

The members of Gethsemane Apostolic Church are taught to live clean lives. Believers' lives will be changed dramatically according to the scripture. Emphasis is given to the witnessing, punctuality and attendance at midweek services.

Friday evening service July 26, 2014 approximately. 100 people.

Church services are held on Wednesdays and Fridays. Members are required to attend midweek services. Bishop McNeil champions the importance and urgency of teaching the gospel.

The outreach ministry of the church trains members and skills for active witnessing, according to the "Great Commission" that Jesus commanded in Matthew 28:19 "Go ye therefore, and teach all nations, baptizing them in the name of the Father and of the Son, and of the Holy Ghost.

Gethsemane Church is fundamentally Apostolic founded on the scripture references Acts 2:32. "This Jesus hath God raised up, whereof we are all witnesses".

Acts 2:33 "Therefore being by the right hand of God exalted and having received of the Father the promise of the Holy Ghost, he hath shed forth this, which ye now see and hear".

Bishop McNeil built a successful trucking business, built and paid for his home in cash. This was done while pastoring his church. God gave him guidance and a personal promise for each project.

Proverbs 3:4-6 "Trust in the Lord with all thine heart, and lean not unto thine own understanding. In all thy ways acknowledge him, and he shall direct thy path."

Greatest struggles in the Ministry.

The first church that he pastored in Lamar, SC, initially rejected the spiritual teaching.

Bishop McNeil faced the challenges of people stealing from the church, resistance to teaching on tithes and living clean separate lives.

Bishop McNeil remained steadfast and the Lord blessed him to remodel the church. He purchased and paid for the first church on Father's Day 1984 for $84,000.

God blessed his ministry to increase and both of his parents joined the church.

Challenges to building construction of Gethsemane Church in Lynchburg, SC.

- Polarization
- Black areas
- Church areas
- White areas
- Gray areas

The political system refused to allow them to build for several years because of the condition of the land. In 2003, the Lord spoke to Bishop McNeil saying go to Bishopville and speak to the Project manager in charge of the permit. The Lord softened his heart and gave him permission to initiate building in 2003.

The county did not provide water, therefore we had to purchase our own septic system. The land was literally a swamp that had to be developed and sustained. God provided the needs at every level. God changed the mind of the commander over time. Nillie, who worked for the Commander, recommended that he buy two acres of land. Henry Hogan agreed to sell the land for $200 per acre. As a result he was to purchase 5 acres. God worked a miracle. In 2004, Bunn Tyson, who owned Allstate, sold them the land on the left side of the church. God gave him favor with the heirs of the land that agreed to purchase the land. God did it! An $8 million church built in 2004, was completely paid for in 2014. Gethsemane Apostolic Church.

Bishop McNeil walked by faith without any financial support from the government, church organization or political support. God is faithful and he is Able!

Ernestine Black

SPECIFIC DETAILS OF EARLY LIFE - Ernestine Black

I was born on December 8, 1942, in Duncan, MS to the late Jim and Martha Watts Black, Sr. I am the youngest of seven children who grew up on a farm. Farming was my father's occupation. My mother was a housewife. My father was uneducated, but had great wisdom. Mother obtained a 9th grade education and was unable to continue any further. They worked together, filling in what was lacking in the other.

I was ill most of the time when I was growing up. I suffered from asthma and had a gastricated stomach. I was healed of asthma after I finished college and began to work. The stomach condition greatly improved, but I still have problems sometimes (depending on what I eat).

My father was a sharecropper until I was about four years old. We then moved to Jonestown, MS where my father had the opportunity to rent. That's when we really began to progress (better life). Work on the farm was hard. We chopped and picked cotton from early morning to late evening. One of the better times during the cotton picking season was when my father would take cotton to the Gin. He would most likely return with fresh Wonder Bread, bologna, and or stage planks (a scalloped cookie with delicious cream on top). We would stop work long enough to eat these goodies, and then return to work.

In addition to cotton, we had a corn crop, and a truck patch, which consisted of watermelon, cantaloupe, sweet potatoes, peanuts, popcorn, etc., and a regular garden. We always had something to do, but still there was time for play and storytelling.

Cattle, hogs, chickens, mules; all had to be cared for. In addition, milk had to be churned, the yard and hen house had to be kept clean, and eggs had to be gathered. Corn had to be shelled to be taken to the mill, corn shelled for chickens, and corn ground for the chicks. Preparing fruit and vegetables for canning took place in the summertime. We had chores to do individually and collectively. Through it all, we were never deprived of obtaining an education. We had split sessions then but when we returned home from school, we had to go to the field.

My Father and mother worked together, but my father worked harder than any of us. He did not have us do anything that he did not do himself. Our schedule was primarily Monday-Saturday until 12:00 noon most of the time. Weekends were short but we were glad to have them. We looked forward to going to town with Daddy on Saturday nights to purchase ice cream bars, and double candy bars.. We three younger children would exchange with each other: Butterfinger, Baby Ruth, and Pay day. (Daddy would give us a small sum of money for working on Saturdays).

The most joyful family time that I had was the 4" of July and Christmas. We would work very hard to reach a certain point so that we could celebrate the day. Sometimes the day would begin with fishing. The entire family would go fishing. Then we would return home and spend the remainder of the day eating and drinking soda pops. Daddy bought ice cream by the crate. Then there were hot dogs with all the trimmings and cookies. Later on in the day, my older brothers would go and play baseball or softball with the boys in the community. We literally ate until we couldn't eat anymore (we didn't have refrigeration until later).

The other special family event was Christmas. Approximately three to five days before this day, mother would begin to prepare the cakes and pies. Eight cakes, different flavors, six lemon pies, about four potato pies and one chocolate pie for my father and I (I do not like lemon pies). Then there was the turkey that had been caged alone and was fed for about two weeks. There was also the ham from the hog that had been killed a few days or weeks earlier. These were prepared on Christmas Eve. I was always in the kitchen with my mother during the preparation. But I regret to this day that I did not observe how she prepared those goodies.

The night before Christmas was extremely exciting, waiting and hoping to receive that special gift that I had been waiting for a long time. Finally, the morning came. When we were all dressed, the day began with family prayer and thanksgiving, and everyone gathered around the tree. Then we would open the gifts. Every child had a shoe box filled with all the Christmas goodies; the same amount in each box. (candy, nuts, raisins, oranges, and apples". At the end of the day, we were stuffed like the turkey that mother had stuffed.

Sundays were spent in church most of the time. It was a "must" that we attend Sunday School, prayer meetings, and worship service. In addition, we had to participate in church activities when asked to do so. Whatever was going on at the church, we had to be there. There were many times when I did not want to go for several reasons: I didn't fit in with the majority, I had inadequate clothing that had to be worn over and over again, and the long hours we had to spend in church. Our pastor invited everyone who could sing or could not sing to sing before he preached. Concerning the clothing, someway, somehow, mother always found a way for us to have new clothes for Easter, even if she had to make them. When I look back, I am glad that my parents required us to go to church, for it was in Sunday School, and mother's reading of the Bible to us, that my love for God's word grew.

As stated earlier, my father was a man of wisdom. He insisted that we all obtain a good education and be able to take care of ourselves. The following are words of wisdom that he instilled in us:

1. Get an education. You cannot make it the way I did.
2. Always pay your debts. If you cannot pay on time, always let the lender know why and how you plan to repay. Repay a little bit at a time if accepted.
3. Always make your own decisions; don't' let others make them for you. You have to live with the decisions you make.
4. Always work for what you want. Do not take from others. If you don't work, you will steal.
5. Don't fight with each other. Always stand together. As long as you stand together, no one can defeat you.
6. Always do what is right. "Right don't wrong nobody".
7. Always do a good day's work for your pay. Do your job, even though the "boss" is not around.
8. Always seek to own and not rent. Something that you own is better than what belongs to someone else (even if it's only two rooms).8"
9. No matter how small your salary might be, always save something out of each payday, even if It is only fifty cents. Keep saving, let it grow, and you will always have something In case of emergencies and other unexpected circumstances.
10. Always reverence God. When storms would arrive, we all had to assemble in the same room and remain quiet.

    A. We have to attend Sunday School every Sunday, and attend church services.
    B. We had to participate in church activities as directed by the Youth Director.
    C. We had to learn our parts; not read them.
    D. We had to respect our elders.

11. Treat everyone right, regardless of the way they treat you. You will be eating "ham and eggs" when they can barely get bread.

EDUCATIONAL BACKGROUND

I was a child that experienced quite a bit of illness during my childhood and up through early adulthood. I suffered severe asthma attacks and had a gastric stomach problem. Through it all, God enabled me to finish High School (Broad Street High, Shelby, MS, 1961). Then I attended Coahoma Jr. College (Coahoma Community College), finishing in 1965 with honors. My major was Business Education (AA Degree). I transferred to Alcorn College (Alcorn State University) in August of the same year. I received the B.S Degree in Business Education in 1965.

I was employed as a Secretary-Teacher in August of the same year at Utica Jr. college (Hinds Community College, Utica Campus). I was the first Secretary of the Vocational-Technical Department. The following summer, I continued my education at the University of Wisconsin, Madison, Wisconsin. At that time, Blacks could not attend White institutions of Higher Learning in the state. The good part about this was that the State of Mississippi, Institutions of Higher Learning paid our expenses to attend school out of state. This resulted in one of the greatest blessings and experiences that could have happened to me. The acquisition of knowledge in my educational field was beyond my expectations. The work was hard and the hours were long, but if I had to do it again (younger), I would. After four (4) summers, I received the M.S Degree in Business Education in 1969, and was inducted into the Delta Pi Epsilon Honor Society.

After receiving the Master's Degree, I was asked and accepted the position of ESEA, Title 1, and Financial Aid Director. After about a year or more, I resigned from these positions. Then I was asked to become Chairperson of the Business Division on the Utica Campus Here again. I was the first to hold this position. I had to set up the curriculum, order equipment and supplies, manage the budget, and supervise two other instructors.

I continued my education beyond the Master's degree, and had acquired about 23 hours. These hours were earned from Mississippi State University, Delta State University, and Jackson State University. Funds were available through the school for instructors to obtain the PhD degree. The only requirement was that after obtaining the degree, you would work for one year at the funding school. I made contact with the Dean at Southern University to pursue a Doctoral Degree. I took the GRE, passed it, and he agreed to accept the hours that I had obtained beyond the Master's to be applied toward this degree. Well, God had other plans. I became ill, had to have surgery that kept me out of work for six (6) weeks. I also experienced a broken toe while playing softball in improper shoes, and survived a tornado that struck the campus. By this time, I realized that God was getting my attention.

SPIRITUAL LIFE PRIOR TO ENCOUNTER WITH JESUS CHRIST

I grew up with God-fearing parents. They reverenced God the best that they knew. We were taken to Sunday School, worship service, and every event that was held at the church. We also had to participate in special event programs like Easter, Children's Day, Mother's Day, etc. In addition, my mother would read the Bible to us. She explained the need for us to believe in Jesus Christ, confess Him, and have eternal life.

At the age of seven (7), during a day time revival service, I was touched by God, however, I did not really understand what was happening. At that time, my elders did not know or understand the Holy Spirit and His operating power in the life of believers therefore, I was not instructed to seek this experience, nor to be submissive to the will and ways of God. ! was baptized and began to love hearing and reading the word of God. My love for the word of God was recognized by my Sunday School teacher. She would sometimes let me teach (if you could call it that) and let me give input concerning the lesson.

All through my early school years, college years, and the beginning of my work years, I continued to attend Sunday School and worship services. I never liked and did not participate in worldly activities, and I found myself being drawn further and further from them. Naturally, this caused me to be mistreated and criticized by my co-workers. Not having a car at that time, I started to attend a church behind the campus where I worked. There I met Pastor A. Stamps, who had returned home to become actively involved in the work of the ministry, and later on became the pastor of this church. He was filled with the Holy Spirit, and was bold in proclaiming the importance of being saved and having this experience. As a result, I began to seek this experience, if indeed, it was real and available to me. It was not very long before I experienced the presence and power of God in my life in ways that I never had before.

MY TESTIMONY SAVING GRACE KNOWLEDGE OF JESUS CHRIST

One Sunday morning, I received a distress call from my sister., (these were frequent and sorrowful). I felt helpless in my ability to help her, to give her words of encouragement and hope, or to offer a positive solution to her problems. I prayed, crying out to God from the depth of my heart saying "if you know me and you know my sister, please come and help us." I made preparations to go to Sunday School. I heard a voice saying, "leave out of the bathroom." As soon as I left, I felt something unusual but pleasant start at the top of my head and traveled down to my feet. I passed out in the spirit. However, I didn't understand it then. When I came to myself, I was praising God in a way that I never had before. I was saying "thank you Jesus, thank you Jesus." Joy overflows my soul, something left me, I felt like a new person. I said that I would not tell anyone about this, but found myself calling my mother, stammering and crying all at the same time. She was glad to hear this great news.

I walked out to go to church and I felt like I was walking about three or four feet above the ground. The grass was the greenest that I have ever seen, and the sky was the bluest blue that I had ever seen. I explained my experience to Pastor Stamps after arriving at the church. He was excited to hear the good news and told me that God had great plans for my life, and further explained to me what I had experienced.

When I returned home, the Holy Spirit directed me to write my sister a letter. it was, I believe, a three page letter written on yellow legal-sized paper. I don't remember all that I wrote because the Holy Spirit was dictating. That letter, she later told me, changed her life.

Jesus began to make Himself known to me in dreams, visions, and through the spoken word. Many things that I saw and heard would come to pass. At first, it somewhat frightened me. I was entering into a spiritual area that I had never been before. A few encounters are as follows: He told me that He was coming back, and that I was to prepare His people to meet Him. (During this time, I stayed in His presence for about three days). One night I spoke in other tongues about half of the night. I saw the Trumpet angels sounding, (Revelation 8-9). I saw the faces of people around the globe. When I asked what it meant, He said, "You must bear the burdens of people." Then I asked, "who will help me bear mine? I was already struggling at this time. He said, "I will help you bear yours."

He (Jesus) instructed me to go on a 5-day fast. I did not eat anything, drink anything, or take anything. I did not experience any hunger or weakness. That was the first and only time that I have gone on a fast that long. Other times have been three days with and without water, but no food.

When I was waiting on the family in Shelby to locate a church home (we had left the previous church) so that I could join them, God showed me a huge umbrella. Then He said, "you must be under the PROTECTIVE COVERING OF A PRAYING CHURCH, PINE GROVE PROGRESSIVE. I was already attending a prayer meeting/ Bible Class there. The late Pastor Clara M. Williams was the pastor, and women in the ministry, especially pastors, were not accepted at that time. Still, I obeyed God. The family did not fight it, but the community did. I did not know that this would be the beginning of the work God had planned for me. The year was 1978.

PHILOSOPHY OF THE HOLY SPIRIT

I believe that the Holy Spirit is the third person in the Godhead: Father, Son, Holy Spirit. He is the Spirit of the living God, sent down to earth on the Day of Pentecost to dwell within the believers. (Acts 2:1-8) His mission is to make us effective witnesses for Christ. Jesus told me, during the early part of my ministry, that He is a perfect gentleman. I believe that what He hears from God, He speaks and acts accordingly. He never glorifies Himself, but glorify Jesus Christ.

I believe that the church is powerless without the working power of the Holy Spirit. He is the Spirit of Truth, therefore, He imparts truth. He is the Spirit of Wisdom, knowledge, and understanding. Therefore, He imparts these things to us. He enables us to do what seems to be impossible. He is the source of power for everything we are able to do in the service of God.

I believe that He is the agent of change. He changes attitudes, and ways of thinking. He changes our perspective of the future, and He will change situations and circumstances. He has been my teacher, leader, and guide. He is my strength when I am weak, my hope, when there seems to be no hope, and my helper when I need it the most. Without Him, I never could have come this far.

I believe that the Holy spirit anoints and appoints believers for service, through the impartation of gifts. These gifts are supernatural, and operated by Him (The Holy Spirit).

1Corinthians 12:28 [28] And God hath set some in the church, first apostles, secondarily prophets, thirdly teachers, after that miracles, then gifts of healings, helps, governments, diversities of tongues.

I believe that all the gifts of the Spirit should be in operation in the church today, including the five—fold ministry gifts

Ephesians 4:11-13 KJV -[11] And he gave some, apostles; and some, prophets; and some, evangelists; and some, pastors and teachers;

[12] For the perfecting of the saints, for the work of the ministry, for the edifying of the body of Christ:

[13] Till we all come in the unity of the faith, and of the knowledge of the Son of God, unto a perfect man, unto the measure of the stature of the fulness of Christ:

PHILOSOPHY OF CHRISTIAN BAPTISM

Believe that every individual who confesses with his/her mouth and believes in the heart that God raised Jesus from the dead, (Romans 10:9), should be baptized. I believe that it symbolizes our turning away from a life of sin to a new life in Christ. I believe that It symbolized our identification with Christ; being baptized into the body of Christ.

I believe that baptism is the solemn rite of our admission in the Christian Church. It shows that we are devoted to Christ and do sincerely believe in Him and admit into the privilege of this identification.

Jesus was baptized, even though He did not need to be. As a man, identifying with us, He followed every mandate given by His Father. Jesus was baptized, being both human and divine. Surely we should be baptized as followers of Him.

THE BOOK OF ACTS

The Book of Acts is a history of the beginning of the New Testament church of the living Christ. I believe that the events recorded are real and should be accepted as truth. It began on the Day of Pentecost. After being on earth for forty (40) days after His resurrection, Jesus departed from this earth. He told His disciples to tarry in the city of Jerusalem until they were endued with power from on high (Luke 24:49). They returned to Jerusalem and spent their time in prayer and supplication with the women and Mary the mother of Jesus. The number was about 120. They were all on one accord and in one place.

Ten days after Jesus left the earth, the Holy Spirit came with the sound of a rushing mighty wind. Divided tongues like fire sat upon each of them and they all were filled with the Holy Spirit and began to speak in other tongues as the Spirit gave them utterance. Those who came from far and near were amazed at this event and wondered what was taking place. Others mocked, saying that they were full of new wine. Peter, now filled with the Holy Ghost, spoke against their mockery. He said that they were not drunk; it being the third hour of the day (9:00 a. m.). But this was fulfillment of the prophecy of the Prophet Joel (Joel 2:28 [28] And it shall come to pass afterward, that I will pour out my spirit upon all flesh; and your sons and your daughters shall prophesy, your old men shall dream dreams, your young men shall see visions:). Peter preached, and 3,000 souls were saved. The followers of Christ met with much persecution, but continued to preach the gospel of our Lord and Savior Jesus Christ. Jesus had told them that the work that He did they would do also and greater work than these. In the name of Jesus they preached the gospel with miracles, signs and wonders following. I believe that the same Holy Spirit that empowered the early church is the same who empowers us today. Many people are just beginning to learn about the mighty working power of the Holy Spirit in the lives of believers. Some believe that what happened then was for that hour and not for us today. They simply do not believe. I believe that the Book of Acts is a pattern for New Testament believers to follow. I believe we, the last day true church, will complete the Book by the addition of another chapter or maybe more. The early church believers gave up all to follow Jesus, and we must do the same.

THE GREAT COMMISSION MATTHEW 28:18-19 -

[18] And Jesus came and spake unto them, saying, All power is given unto me in heaven and in earth.

[19] Go ye therefore, and teach all nations, baptizing them in the name of the Father, and of the Son, and of the Holy Ghost:

I believe that the great commission Jesus gave to his disciples then is the same for the church today. Our number one priority should be to preach the gospel of our Lord and Savior Jesus Christ; winning souls for the kingdom of God. We baptize them in the name of the Father, Son, and Holy Spirit. We are to teach them to be obedient to all things that Christ has commanded. I believe that we should not only teach them, but live what we teach. I believe that true believers should not only be followers of Christ, but also imitators of Him, Ephesians 5:1 - Be ye therefore followers of God, as dear children;

I believe that Jesus is with us as He said, "I am with you always," to enable us to be successful in this great undertaking. The power of Christ, through the Holy Spirit's power, is greater than the kingdom of darkness ruled by Satan. I believe that salvation through Christ should be offered to all regardless of race, creed, or color. I believe that the great commission applies to all believers, and not just ministers. The responsibility for getting the invitation to others should be done by all. Everyone should help in every possible way to evangelize the world according to our abilities and directions from God.

HOW AND WHEN DID I KNOW THAT GOD HAD CALLED ME TO PREACH

I received several calls from God before I accepted the call to preach. The first call was in 1978. I was home for a visit with my parents before returning to work. One night, while in bed, a white cloud appeared at the back of my head. It was small at the top but was wide at the bottom. (I was not knowledgeable about God and clouds at the time.) A voice spoke to me out of the cloud and said, "go ye into all the world and minister". I said, "to whom"? He said, "to my people". When I awakened the next morning, I had the strange feeling that I had been visited by an unfamiliar force; a good one. So I asked God if He would visit me during the night. The Holy Spirit started at the top of my head and down through my body. I was overpowered by the Spirit and spoke in another language. God told me some things that I was to do; some have come to pass and others are yet to come. I was in that state most of the morning. However, I told myself that He was not calling me to preach because He did not use the word preach at that time. I was teaching His word, and I felt that that was what I was to do.

God did not call me again until 1980. My pastor had asked me to be the speaker for a special program we were having. After I spoke, she asked people to come around and greet me; to wish me well. As some touched me, the Spirit of God came upon them. It was a great move of God that surprised me. When I returned home, changed my clothing, and in the process of combing and setting my hair, I told God that I had done my best to represent Him that day. Then I heard Him say, "this is the beginning of many, many more. You are to declare my words to the nations". Again. I was overpowered by the Holy spirit. Again, I told myself that He still did not tell me to preach.

One Wednesday night during prayer service, the Holy Spirit was present, and He fell upon me in a mighty way. This was June, 1982. I was seated on the front bench and fell to the floor. I was aware of my pastor and others praying over me. There was praying and singing going on at the same time. When! came to myself, these words came out of my mouth: The Spirit of the Lord is upon me because He has anointed me to preach the gospel. I heard the word PREACH. That night I accepted the call to preach the gospel. I preached my first sermon the same year, and was ordained the fifth Sunday night in June, 1983.

Why did I wait so long? I really did not want to do this, but if God wanted me to do it, I had to be sure that it was He speaking to me. I knew how difficult it would be for a female to undertake such a task. My pastor was a female, so I knew firsthand what to expect. Then, too, I had heard about the hardships that other women in ministry had experienced. I just wanted to be sure. If God ordained me. He would sustain me. I'm still here.

HOW AND WHEN DID I KNOW THAT GOD HAD GIVEN ME A DIVINE ASSIGNMENT TO PASTOR?

As the late Pastor William's health began to fail, she announced to the congregation that I was to become her assistant. No one objected to my being placed in this position. At this time, I was already serving as Church Secretary, Bible Class teacher, and Sunday School teacher. f also ministered every second night at 7:00 p.m. This continued for several years.

As Pastor William's health continued to decline, she asked me to carry on when she was unable to attend and function in her given position. On May 27, 2007, she felt well enough to attend church(she had not been since October, 2006). On this Sunday in May, she spoke these words to the congregation, (She later said that she did not know that she was going to say what she said); "Minister Black is now your pastor. She is your pastor and my pastor. You are to obey her, follow her, and pray for her. She will not lead you wrong. She is concerned about every aspect of your life; the way you dress, your health, and your soul. She will give you the truth. You might not like it but it is the truth. She will not lead you wrong." I served as pastor until her death in August, 2009. The time span was four years and eleven months.

After her death, I was going to call a meeting for us to come together to discuss how we would go about selecting another pastor (I was not taking for granted that they would accept what she had said). Naturally, we were going to pray. I had decided that if the majority decision was someone I could not work with, I would leave in peace. Before I could call the meeting, a few of the members (leaders) had come together and decided to call their own meeting. They said that I had already been serving as pastor, they knew me as opposed to bringing in someone else that they did not know. Having different ministers to come in would possibly divide the congregation. They called for a vote and I was unanimously elected pastor of the Pine Grove Progressive Church. The date was August 23, 2009. I was installed on March 28, 2010.

After all of this, ! was not satisfied that this was the will of God for me (I had not heard Him say PASTOR). I sought for an assurance from Him in prayer. A few days later, I opened my Bible to study. It was a Bible that someone has given me with my name engraved on it, (ERNESTINE BLACK). Then I heard the Spirit say, Pastor Ernestine Black, time to move on, things will begin to get rough. Pastoring is different from being an Evangelist, so I began to wonder if I was clear on this matter of being a pastor. On July 18, 2015, I heard the Spirit say, "you are a pastor."

God has proven himself to me. He has been with me through the good times and the bad times. Out of all the Devil's tricks and attacks, He has enabled me to stand. I have not been defeated and I never will be defeated as long as I remain with Him.

HOW AND WHEN DID I KNOW THAT GOD HAD ASSIGNED ME TO BUILD THIS CHURCH?

"The late Pastor Williams and I had been discussing the need for expansion of the church. We had thought about adding on and had someone come in to see if it was possible or feasible to do so. He told us that he did not think it was a good idea. I agreed. but the Pastor was somewhat reluctant. After sharing with her some things that God had spoken to me about, she agreed that we should make plans for the building of a new church. The following words that God spoke to me let me know that the building of the new church was assigned to me

1. August 21, 1998 — God showed me in a dream that the church was being rebuilt. The ground had been cleared off around it. I saw one side that was partially completed but was not shaped like the present church.
2. July 9, 2003 —it was in my garden meditating on the conversation that Pastor Williams and I had had about adding on to the present church. The Holy Spirit said, " no man puts a piece of new cloth on an old garment." After this, we purchased a CD and allowed it to grow. In addition to the CD, we started a Building Fund and did not use any of the funds for anything else.
3. July 12. 2003 —1 was at the church praying. I heard the Spirit say. "I am going to build the church."
4. November 25, 2004 — The Holy Spirit spoke, "the church is to be built debt free." I asked, how? (We were thinking about borrowing the money). I said, "you will have to provide," He said, "I will provide all you need:"
5. June 2, 2007 I heard the Spirit say, "Mr. Ross (our contractor) is going to build the church at a reasonable price.
6. He will not know why he is doing it." (The Lord expressed this later in other words)
7. December 23, 2009, 12:00 p.m. — The Spirit spoke. "It is time to build the church." We did not have all the needed funds. We had decided that we would have most of the needed funds before the project began. Naturally, the members felt that we should go ahead and borrow the money. However, I remembered what He had said in 2004.
8. April, 2010 — The Blueprint has been drawn up, and we proceeded with the planning preparation stage. After this, the members decided that all future decisions would be made by Pastor Black and Deacon Trueville Black. (He was the only deacon at this time).
9. May 29, 2010 — Ground Breaking ceremony was held.
10. August, 2010—Mr. Ross began construction, after clearing off the land. The funding was to be obtained through tithe and offerings. We could not ask for donations, sell dinner plates. hold raffles. etc. God said that He wanted the finances to be provided through what He blessed us with.

EVANGELIZING THE MEMBERS OF THE CHURCH

Among the leadership, nothing was ever hidden from the members. There were no hidden agendas or undercover activities. The majority of the members did their best in hearing and following instructions. They were told that if this project was to come to completion, it would be the hand of Almighty God and our following His leadership. They were encouraged not to listen to the negative talk that came from outsiders. Outsiders were saying that it could not be done because the membership was too small. Members were reminded that with God, all things are possible.

Members are taught to tell about the goodness of the Lord, but to never take credit for God's works. The members were encouraged to invite family and friends to worship service, Sunday School, Bible class and other church activities, and reminding them that the way they lived would have more of an impact on others than what they said.

Members are being taught the importance of not neglecting to assemble ourselves together, and that God is to be honored, feared, thanked, and praised at all times. That the Word of God is to be studied, meditated on, believed, and lived by. Also, an on-going relationship with Jesus Christ is the most important thing in one's life.

WHAT I DID TO MOBILIZE AND INVOLVE THE MEMBERS AND THE COMMUNITY IN THE BUILDING OF THE CHURCH?

THE MEMBERS: It was not difficult at all to get the members involved in the building project. Everyone desired and saw the need to have more space and to be more comfortable when we came together. Then, too, we were/are known as a "praying church" and we always prayed about matters that concerned the church (As a group). Another factor, I believe, that resulted in the full cooperation of the members was their confidence in the leadership. They believed that their leaders had a close relationship with God and followed His leadership. No one objected to the amount that was suggested that each member was to pay ($1000) every four months and then it was reduced to twice per year. All were not able to do this but did not fight against the proposal. They did what they could, even those on fixed income or limited income. No one was forced to do beyond their ability.

Another factor was that everyone was involved in the planning phase from the very beginning. They were involved with the blueprint and other decisions like the colors, materials, furnishings, etc.

THE COMMUNITY: The community, as a whole, was against the church from the very beginning. Since God said that we could not solicit funds, we couldn't ask them for donations. Many said that there was no way that a few members like us could build a church. So they watched and waited for the church to fail. They did not realize that if God is for you. who can be. against you. (Romans 8:31) There were a few who gave us small donations for special occasions but not for the building project.

MY GREATEST STRUGGLES IN THE MINISTRY

My greatest struggles in the ministry were:

1. Always facing the opposition that women are not supposed to preach. The church that I now pastor started out as a Baptist church. Also, most of the churches in this area are Baptist. The leaders, as well as others,

spread their hatred and resentment of women, therefore, we were hindered from ministering in many places. They would go as far to say that if anyone went to hear a female preach, they would go to hell. This rejection came from both males and females. I had three strikes against me: female, single, and black.

2. I struggled to impart the Gospel of our Lord and Savior Jesus Christ to a people who were dull of hearing, hard to understand spiritual things, bound by customs and traditions, the inability to understand and appreciate the fact that there are some people in the world who are genuine, and have their best interest at heart. It was/is a struggle to show them that God has provided better things for them through His Son, Jesus Christ, and that they do not have to live the way they were/are living. Much later, God let me know that I was sent here to break up fallow ground, to shine light in a dark place, and to show them the reality that God is alive and well, and loves them more than they can ever think.

3. I struggled to get past the betrayal of those that I trusted to be my friends, when in truth, they were harming me behind my back. (I thought that people valued friendship the way that I do).

4. I struggled to get past the persecutions that I endured merely because I made the choice to follow Christ, which required me to live a different type of lifestyle. Some even ventured to say that no one can live like I live so I must be hiding behind some type of secret sin. I have been accused of being a lesbian, taking advantage of mentally challenged individuals, taking all the members' money, and taking money from the elderly and the sick. (I was the primary caregiver for our late pastor. I have not taken anything from anyone).

5. I struggled for a while getting past the things that people said to me; even some relatives. Some of the sayings were in reference to the ministry. "If that is what you want to do, then…" It was not something that I wanted to do, but what God wanted me to do. They couldn't understand that You are Miss "goody-two-shoes" because I would not engage in worldly activities like they did. When I was filled with the Holy Spirit, some said that I had lost my mind. God does not call women to preach.

6. During the 90's, about ten years, especially the later part, I struggled with balancing the work of the ministry. a full time job. and the care of my ailing parents. At my church I was a Bible Class teacher. Sunday School teacher. Secretary. and Asst. pastor. I was also Bible Class teacher for two other churches

I would travel 142 miles one way to get to my parent's home. (This was done every other week and sometimes every week). I prepared food for them, taking it with me in freezer chests. I left work on Friday evening, and arrived there just before dark. After unpacking, I would take care of their personal needs, clean the house, and prepare freshly cooked meals. I would go to bed late and rise up early. Leaving early Sunday morning, I would make my way back here to fulfill my church obligations. Many times, I barely had time to change clothing and get to church on time. This included preaching as well as other duties. I would be extremely tired to the point that I felt like I could not go any further. Sometimes, I would fall asleep while driving, but God always awakened me just in time. How I kept up this pace, only God knows. I told God that I just couldn't do this anymore. But He showed me how to better balance my load, and gave me the strength to carry on.

My father passed, February 1996 at the age of 94. After he passed, my mother was left alone. She had lost most of her sight and was unwilling to come and live with me. (she was not familiar with my home). We, her children, concluded that it was best for her to stay in her own home, and that we would do what we could to care for her. Still, there was no relief for me; she had to be cared for. This continued very well until she had a fall that she could not explain. She was hospitalized, but was recovering well. However, she could no longer live alone. I asked God to relieve me of some of my responsibilities: Take a leave of absence from my job, as well as a leave of absence from ministry. I could not see no way around this. God did not release me, but He sent us a loving caring caregiver who was willing to stay with her during the week. We only had to take care of her on weekends. I had no idea that God would make such provisions for us. We had said that no one would be willing to stay in the rural area with an old lady. God always has a plan. While we are trying to figure it out, He has already worked it out. Mother passed away in January 1999 at the age of 90. I can truly say that God was with me all the way. All of this with limited resources.

7. I struggled with my own inward battles.
   - Am I really in the place where God wants me to be?
   - Am I doing all that He has ordained for me to do?
   - Have I spoken anything at any given time that He did not tell me to say or do? (Sometimes the other spirit interferes with what God is saying).
   - I have had doubts (and still have some doubts) about my ability, capability, understanding, etc., to be a leader of the people of God.

MY EARLY YEARS IN THE MINISTRY

My early years in the ministry I would say was a mixture of the good, the bad, and the ugly. The bad.

1. There was always the rejection of women in the ministry.
2. I was accused by certain women in a certain denomination that I was aspiring for the ministry, and women were never called by God. (I was attending a community Bible Class with them at this time). One of these women invited me to her home to convince me that women were not to preach. When she sent for me, I did not know that this was what she wanted.
3. When our members would fellowship with other churches and made announcements about upcoming events in our church, some pastors would make a mockery of us when our names were mentioned. Naturally, our members were hurt and saddened. We had told them not to defend us. Later on. one of these pastors traveled out of state. but did not return alive. Another became ill. legs were amputated, and later died. Another died also. but I never knew the cause.
4. We heard that a few anti-women ministers had planned to visit the churches where females were pastoring and send us on our way. However, they never came to our church. Thank God.

God had a few male pastors who stood by us. Also, I had the support and encouragement of my pastor, the late Clara M. Williams. These male pastors opened their doors for me to minister. Two of them asked me to become their Bible Class teacher. I was also asked to preach for different events, conduct revivals, co-ordinate Women Conferences, and co-sponsor prayer conferences. All this did not happen at once, but over a period of time.

During the early years of ministry, God dealt with me in a different way than he does now. I worked full time, taught Bible Classes and preached. Messages and Bible lessons came to me easier. It seemed as if the Holy Spirit was more active. I did not realize that I was being prepared for the more difficult days ahead. I had to learn to trust and depend on God more for every situation and under every circumstance. (I still have some difficulty in this area).

HOW WAS THE WORK AND THE BUILDING
OF THE CHURCH FINANCED?

In 2003, we started a Building Fund for the express purpose of building a new Church. We did not use the funds for any other purpose. We met and agreed that each family would pay $1000 per quarter. That proved to be a bit much for most, so it was reduced to twice yearly. Those who could, paid more; others paid what they could.

In June 2006, we decided to move $85,000 from the Building Fund and put it in a CD account. By the time we were ready to build. it had increased to more than $95,000. There were 12 members who consistently paid (tithe and offerings), three honorary members, and three family members who contributed on a regular basis. Occasionally, a very few friends would give us small donations. We were thankful because every cent given was a help. There were also some former members (family) who had left and moved to another state. They heard about the building project and sent no less than $500 several times.

We received $3,460.42 from our insurance company to replace the roof in the old building. We patched the roof and used the money for the construction of the new building.

There was also an anonymous donor (Details given under miraculous events). The work was done under the contracted leadership of Mr. Albert Ross. His work was far and beyond our expectations. GOD DID IT.

THE LARGEST CONTRIBUTION AND THE TOTAL
AMOUNT OF THE CHURCH BUILT

The largest contribution was $30,000.00 The total amount of the church was $271 819.10

The total cost was $394,000.00 close to $400,000 due to additional things.

Building 1, our old church (from history) - The congregation was very small. Other than the pastor and his wife, there were two other families. However, there were others in the community that attended the church.

The Ministry

The ministry consisted of Bible Study, Sunday School, and worship service. Also, Rev. Miller visited and sick and shared what resources he had with others who were in need.

The Building — (from the History) — The original building was built in 1958 by the founder, Rev. Leon Miller. He said that the Lord told him to build Him a house. He acquired the materials from an old Methodist church built in 1892. The church was no longer in use and those around it wanted it moved. A friend of Rev.

Miller was paid $20.00 to move the church. Rev. Miller paid him $200.00 for the building. The other materials came from timber from his own property. He was offered $500.00 for the bell, but refused to sell it. (The bell is still with the church}.

Rev. Miller built one room where everything took place. Gradually, he added two more rooms, and built a small area for the pulpit. There were no inside restrooms or plumbing. The outside was covered with black tar paper.

In 1975. Pastor Clara M. Miller Williams was elected pastor, after serving in her brother's place for eleven (11) months during his illness. During her administration many additions and repairs were made to the church.

SUPERNATURAL PROVISIONS THE LORD MANIFESTED

The place where the church is now located was owned by some individuals who did not live on it or keep it up. It was overgrown with trees and bushes. Then, too. individuals were using it as a garbage dump. The lot was located behind the old church.

One day I received a call from the owner asking for me. She had been told that I was the person to speak to because she wanted to sell the lot. They had no plans for it. Since it was located behind the old church, she thought that we would be interested in purchasing it. I told her "yes". We met at the lawyer's office, transferred the deeds, and paid all fees. Everything moved along smoothly. She only charged us for what she had paid for the lot many years earlier.

Our plans for the new church was to tear down the old church and build the new church in its place. When our contractor came to do measurements in accordance with the blueprint, he told us that the space would not accommodate the new building. God knew this, but we didn't, and had supernaturally made the lot behind the church available to us.

As our contractor, Mr. Ross, cleared the lot and packed soil, he called for a soil inspector to inspect the soil. This was necessary in order to determine the suitability of construction on it. The inspector said that there was a problem with the soil that could likely hinder the construction process. We (the church) came together and prayed. Mr. Ross continued to clear and pack the soil. When the inspector came the second time, he said that the soil was ok. Again, God did something supernaturally with the soil. The construction process continued.

As the construction progressed, God told me that the church was to have Ram's Horn columns instead of the regular brick columns. THIS WAS NOT IN THE BUDGET. Then after the electrical wiring had been installed, God showed me that He wanted a chandelier over the pulpit. THIS WAS NOT IN THE BUDGET. Our contractor has to purchase a culvert to take care of the water flow. THIS, TOO, WAS NOT IN THE BUDGET. We discussed how we would pay for the changes and additions. I suggested going into my personal savings account, and my nephew, Deacon Black, said he would help. He did not want me to go into my savings account. He believed that God would provide. I don't know how, but the funds were there when needed.

SOME MIRACULOUS EVENTS JEHOVAH JIREH -GOD PROVIDED GENESIS 22:14

1. The old church had lost some shingles due to a storm. Our insurance company investigated, and concluded that we needed a new roof. They paid us the full price for a new roof because it was leaking in several places. Since we were going to build, we decided to patch the roof and put the money on the new building. I was afraid that the roof would not hold up until we were ready to move. During that time, we had a series of heavy, hard rain. After these downpours, I would go to the church expecting to see new and or old leaks. To my amazement, not one leak occurred during the duration of the building project. God proved himself to be our Jehovah Jireh; He provided.

2. When the construction of the new church began, we did not have all the funds that were needed. Our contractor has agreed to do certain portions of the project, and then receive payment. Every time we needed to make a payment, the funds were there. This continued until it was time for the last payment. We had exhausted practically all funds. Then we received a donation of $10,000 from a donor who did not want to be known. The $10,000 was the exact amount we needed to complete the last payment, (God provided).

3. One day, our church secretary and I were looking for some classroom furniture for our primary group. A lady that we had never seen or met before came up to us and asked if we were looking for tables and chairs. Our reply was "yes". She told us that she had a folding table with matching chairs at her house. She had no use for them, and all we had to do was come and get them; no charge. When the ones who came to get them arrived, she not only gave us the table and chairs, but four (4) office chairs that only need some upholstering. There was no charge for any of this. Again, God provided.

THE RESPONSE OF BELIEVERS, PEOPLE, AND CONGREGATION AT THE OUTSET OF MY MINISTRY

1. BELIEVERS: Some really believed that I had been called by God and responded in a positive way. Others were reluctant, but did not fight against me. God had prepared the hearts of a few people, I believe, in order for them to believe. One said to me after I announced my calling, "what have you been waiting on? Saw this some time ago." Another said that they knew it but it was not for them to tell me. I needed to know it for myself. Another said that they saw me in the Spirit dressed in white, similar to the attire that I wore when I preached my first sermon. Two others said that they saw a halo over my head, once when I was ministering, and once when I was attending a church service at another church.

2. PEOPLE: This one person in particular, supposed to have been a believer, asked me to meet with her one day. She told us that she had heard that I was aspiring for the ministry. At that time, I was attending a neighborhood Bible Study where she was one of the teachers. At the same time, I was also attending Bible Class at the church which I now pastor. This individual bluntly told me that God did not call women to preach, and that I was being misled, misguided, and misdirected. Women were to keep silent in the

church, quoting from 1 Corinthians 14:34 [34] Let your women keep silence in the churches: for it is not permitted unto them to speak; but they are commanded to be under obedience as also saith the law. She missed the fact that Paul said, "your women', and not all women.

Many people in this area had been taught that God does not call women to preach. Naturally their response was negative. They would look at me as if I were an alien from another planet. They would whisper and laugh especially if their pastors made a negative comment about women in the ministry. Some were told to never attend a service where I was to minister, even going as far as to say that if they did, they would go to Hell. In spite of all this, some paid no attention to what was being said, and gave their support.

3. CONGREGATION: Most of the congregation had witnessed the way God had been dealing with me prior to my acceptance. I believe that most of them believed that this was the hand of God, and they embraced It. As far as I know, no one questioned my calling, and supported me.

MY VISION FOR THE MINISTRY, FOR THE PEOPLE

At the beginning of the ministry that God called me into, Jesus gave me a series of promises (prophetic words) that He said would be accomplished during the ministry. I have proposed in my heart that I will do my best not to hinder what He desires to be accomplished through me. These promises are in keeping with what He said in John 14:12: "He that believeth on me, the works that I do shall he do also; and greater works than these. ..." I visualize that the true last day church will add another chapter to the Book of Acts. In doing so, we will carry out the Great Commission, bringing souls into the kingdom of God, and God being glorified in all things.

As I continue to teach and preach the word of God, I believe that the membership will continue to increase, as God begins to perform signs and wonders among us.

Congregations will reflect Jesus Christ as they continue to see God, His will and His ways. Those who are not saved will be saved, sanctified, and filled with the Holy Spirit. That those who are in the community will become our friends as we continue to reach out to them with the love of God, and showing our love for one another. (When there is a disaster, illness, or death in the community, we always reach out to them, as well as those beyond the community.

I do not have specific plans at this time. I have always sought God in all things, and continue to rely on His guidance and directions. I don't want to lay behind Him or run out before Him. I Just want to be in His will, do His will, and abide in His will at all times.

CHRONOLOGICAL EVENTS RELATED TO MY MINISTRY

1. August, 1978 - First call into the ministry: "Go ye into all the world and minister." I asked, to whom? He said my people. United with Pine Grove Progressive church, October, 1978. God told me that I had to be

2. Under the protective covering of a praying church, a Prophet told me that I was never to leave this church unless God told me.

3. November, 1980 Second call. "You are to declare my word unto the nations".

4. June, 1982 — Accepted call: I heard myself saying, after I was slain in the Spirit, "the Spirit of the Lord is upon me because He has anointed me to preach the gospel.

5. Preached first sermon, licensed, August 15, 1982.

6. Ordained, July 31, 1983.

7. Conducted my first revival at Pine Grove Progressive, September 17-21, 1984.

8. August 13, 1990, I heard, "do the work of an Evangelist, make full proof of your ministry'.

9. I retired from work at the end of December, 2000. On November 11, 2000, God had said
   To me it is your time to go higher in the Lord. This is your new beginning.

10. September, 2013 — Our revival speaker was a guest minister from out of town. She preached the word, and God worked on my heart. The second night, I was slain in the Spirit, and the Spirit remained with me all the week. By the end of the week, it was prophesied that I would be given two anointings; Prophetic and Healing. That following Sunday, the Spirit spoke to me personally, verifying what had been said. On September 22, 2013, I heard Prophetess Black. God gave me this title, however, I do not use it. I prefer to let the work speak for itself. On September 25, 2013, I heard the two anointings: prophetic and healing. Since that time, messages have become more frequent and numerous. Some manifested healings are on the increase among those who believe.

Dr. G. Yvette Boatwright – Jesus Ministries

  I was born in Darlington, South Carolina in the late 1940's to Margaret & Hubert Boatwright. I was the second child of seven. One son, a set of twin girls and one adopted daughter, the only child of my mother's deceased sister, completed our family. My father is a second generation, mortician funeral home entrepreneur, world war II Veteran actively involved in his two funeral businesses, we worshiped at Bethel AME Church. My mother worked part time in her family's restaurant/motel business during our early years. She transitioned at midlife to full-time homemaker and family anchor and transitioned to the Lord in 2007, after becoming incapacitated for one and a half years.

  We were blessed with a strong supportive family of unity Christianity, education and wholesome values. I graduated from Bethune Cookman College - Daytona Beach, Florida at the age of 21. I began my adult life in Chicago working as a teacher, youth worker and partying etc.

  Prior to attending college, my spiritual life consisted of church, singing in the choir and nightly prayers. I confessed to Christ at an early age and joined Bethel AME Church. I stopped attending church during college.

Navigating my life in Chicago was daunting without Christ. I experienced a broken toxic relationship and two serious automobile accidents. During a 5 year period after college, experiencing family problems, apathy, relationship problems, serious illness of my mother, etc... humbled me. Thus, I began to read my Bible daily, and disassociated with friends.

The Lord began to draw me, saved and filled me with the Holy Spirit. My personal life was transformed through great deliverance and healing in all areas. I became a member of Monument of Faith Church and enrolled at Moody Bible Institute. My Spiritual life journey began by teaching Sunday School and coordinating the Youth Department at North Wells Gospel Mission, where I was ordained as an evangelist in 1989, functioning as an unofficial-active member of the church. The nursing home ministry began as a practical Christian requirement at Moody Bible Institute currently having a ministry at Kenwood Nursing Home monthly since 2005.

Principles of Sanctifications

Ministry was guided by my Spiritual Mother Green, based on 50+ years of evangelistic service, which included preaching, teaching, hospital ministry, and 24-hour prayer room for the Lord. Fortunately, she taught me, counseled, provided shut-ins, and weekly all night prayer sessions. Mother Green and her prayer warriors facilitated routine sessions of Tarrying for the Filling of the Holy Ghost with the evidence of Speaking in Tongues according to Acts 2:8:" But ye shall receive power after that the Holy Ghost is come upon you; and ye shall be witnesses unto me both in Jerusalem and in all Judea, and in Samaria and unto the uttermost part of the earth."

During this season, many believers were taught biblical principles of salvations, prayers, sanctification, and serving the Lord Jesus. Jesus Ministry began; Jesus sent his disciples out in groups of two. Thus, I began bedside ministry with Evangelist Sereta Deal, one of my Sunday School students and member of North Wells Gospel ministries. For many years, we ministered regularly after work on Monday.

The Personal Evangelistic Ministry there produced souls that accepted the Lord Jesus. Literature was distributed, and Back Sliders were restored. This Evangelistic endeavor increased our strength, faith and determination to serve the Lord Jesus Christ.

The Ministry of the Twelve - Mark 6:7-8

Evangelistic ministry continued as the Holy Spirit led and directed us to various individuals, members of the church, prisons, homes, and hospitals.

Evangelism at Cook County Hospital:

Evangelistic training and ministry began in 1980 under the auspices of Chaplin Pembrooke, who became members of The Light Bearers association.

Chaplin Pembrooke, was an anointed, experienced man of God. He thought and demonstrated the Christian applications of leading souls to Christ at a critical stage of life. Catastrophe, illness and trauma brings mankind face to face to mortality and eternity, essential questions of life "What Shall I do with Jesus?" We ministered the plan of Salvation according to Roman Road. In this environment evangelistic efforts and results became fluid and fast; The Holy Spirit moved on consistently, reclaimed, healed and delivered many souls.

Meeting God in the Broken Places - Jesus Ministry

Missionary Catherine Scott, Pastor Momory Deal and his Wife Deborah Deal former Sunday School members trained at Cook County Hospital with Chaplin Pembrooke and joined the Evangelistic team. The Lord opened an effective door of opportunity at Kenwood Nursing Home February 2004.

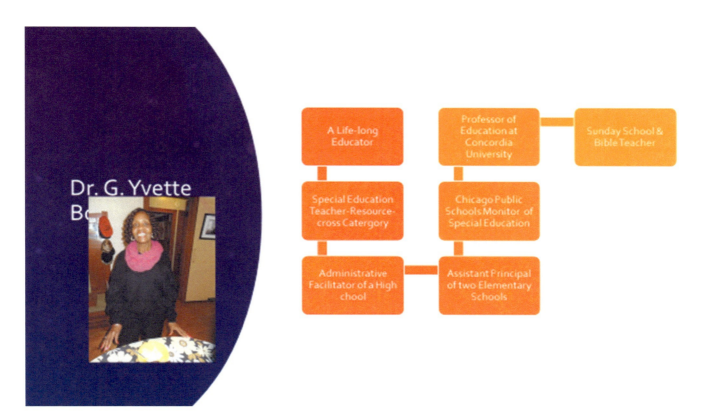

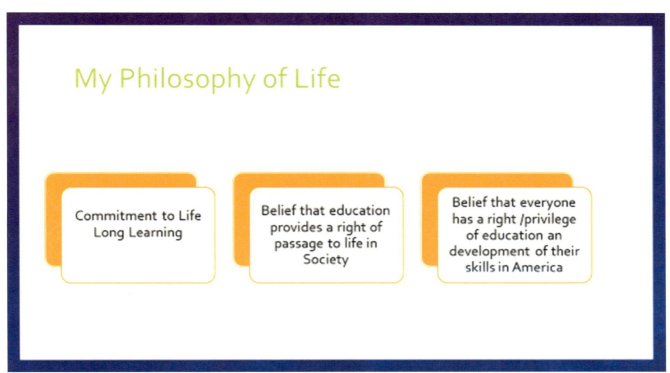

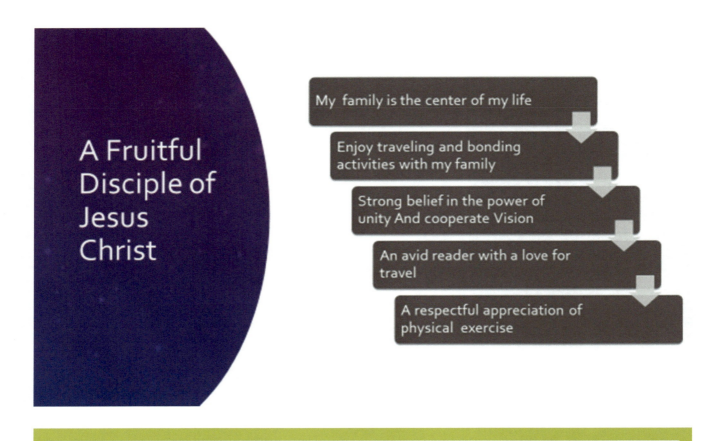

A Fruitful Disciple of Jesus Christ

- My family is the center of my life
- Enjoy traveling and bonding activities with my family
- Strong belief in the power of unity And cooperate Vision
- An avid reader with a love for travel
- A respectful appreciation of physical exercise

Fishers of Men

- Provide personalized emotional support to the Clients in various institutions
- Facilitate connections with a local church as needed
- Provide personal items, treats and celebrations, ex., Christmas gifts, musical presentations
- Develop relationship with Jesus Christ ,family and interpersonal relationships

\

Matthew 4: 18-19 KJV

"And Jesus walking by the Sea of Galilee saw two brothers called Peter and Andrew, his brother casting a net into the sea, for they were fishers. And he saith unto them follow me and I will make you a fisher of men."

The Lord blessed me with the teaching of ministry during a Practical Christian Work Weekly as a responsibility for each born again Christian. This fact was exemplified and supported by my spiritual mothers; Evangelist Betty Green. A powerful anointed evangelist, Mother Green taught me how to walk into the Beauty of Holiness Supporting my personal life, as I endeavored to integrate teaching in the Chicago Public School while continuing educational pursuits.

During my time of emptiness, failure, confusion and pain Jesus drew me unto himself. Jesus spoke these words: "I am, come that you might have life the Lord baptized me in the precious Holy Ghost" on Thursday September 17, 1971.

It happened about six-o-clock in the home of a sister that I met at Monument of Faith Evangelist Church. After fasting and staying home from work one day, Jesus baptized me in the Holy Ghost with evidence of speaking in tongues! Totally engulfed in the spirit for hours I experienced transition to a place of supernatural peace! Never desired to return or go back!

This supernatural peace continued to overshadow me for days as I returned to my normal life. My life involved teaching school, attending church and bible classes at Monument of Faith and prayer meetings with my Godmother.

- Old things passed away, therefore I changed home.
- When a person encounters Jesus: A change occurs.
- Encountering Jesus Changes a Life
- Jesus Christ has Transforming Power

My flesh had to become subject to God's Word, no longer committing fornication. Jesus SAVES, SANCTIFIES and SATISFIES if you desire it.

James 4:8 KJV [8] Draw nigh to God, and he will draw nigh to you. Cleanse your hands, ye sinners; and purify your hearts, ye double minded.

There is no temptation taken from you, but much that is common to man - God will also make a way of escape.

James 4:10 KJV [10] Humble yourselves in the sight of the Lord, and he shall lift you up.

A new born again Christian must be willing to forsake sin and surrender a life unto God!

I beseech you brethren by the mercies of God that you present your bodies a Living Sacrifice – Holy acceptable unto God, which is your reasonable service and be not conformed to this world, but be transformed by the renewing of your mind.

Journey Through The Wilderness

Spiritual Boot Camp: An experience with Jesus changes a person, a visible change occurs that others can see! Not education, wealth or people.

1971 Jesus equips his servants to complete the work that he assigns to our hands for the perfecting of the church.

The Power of the Holy Spirit: operative definition. It is a crucial element for the life of every Christian, research indicates that ordinary people accomplish extraordinary work in the ministry when they function more in the power of the Holy Spirit. (Acts 2:8 KJV)

Proverbs 3:5, 6 KJV

⁵ Trust in the LORD with all thine heart; and lean not unto thine own understanding.

⁶ In all thy ways acknowledge him, and he shall direct thy paths.

Spiritual Gifts and The "Priesthood of All Believers" are necessary: Christians must be taught that spiritual gifts are necessary, Christians must be able to recognize and use Spiritual Gifts.

Finding God's Plan for my Life!

Therefore, if any man be in Christ he is a new creature and old things are passed away, behold all things become new. Apostle Paul wrote, if a man be in Christ he is a new creature, (II Corinthians 5:17 KJV)

Getting to know the Holy Spirit, surrendering to the Lord Jesus Christ and filling the baptism of the Holy Ghost, he led me to learn more about the word of God. Enrolled in evening school at Moody Bible Institute, Chicago Illinois, I learned amazing principles and promises of God.

Quality Characteristic Ministry

The roll of the church in Christian leadership is to help its members identify their gifts and to integrate them into their areas of giftedness.

Current research demonstrated a highly significant relationship between "gift-orientation" and highly effective Christians. There is evidence that when personal ministry matches the believers gift, the result is personal joy in Christian living.

The Lord filled me with the Holy Ghost evidence of speaking in tongues, gifts of prophesying, teaching and preaching. In 1974, the journey began at Monument of Faith Evangelistic Church, leadership of Apostle Richard D. Henton Worldwide Evangelistic Ministry. I became a member attending weekly services, experiencing personal deliverance from habits of drinking, and worry. The ministry taught me the principles of living a Holy Life in a contemporary world. Simultaneously the Lord equipped me to learn and apply His word by studying at Moody Bible Institute and teaching at North Wells Gospel Mission.

Moody Bible Institute placed me at North Wells as a requirement for my practical educational component. The Lord had a purpose and a greater spiritual plan. At North Wells, I served as a Sunday school teacher, Youth Department leader and developed an effective prayer group. During this period of 20 years, I attended both churches, North Wells in the morning Sunday services and Monument of Faith began on Sunday at 2:00pm and at 6:00pm. The Lord arranged the schedule for His purpose, developing my life and ministry.

Jesus calls us and the Holy Spirit draws us into salvation and ministry for the Kingdom of God.

Jesus said to Peter, "if you love me, feed my sheep."

Scripture John 21:15, 16 KJV

[15] So when they had dined, Jesus saith to Simon Peter, Simon, son of Jonas, lovest thou me more than these? He saith unto him, Yea, Lord; thou knowest that I love thee. He saith unto him, Feed my lambs.

[16] He saith to him again the second time, Simon, son of Jonas, lovest thou me? He saith unto him, Yea, Lord; thou knowest that I love thee. He saith unto him, Feed my sheep.

Practical Christian Principles taught by Precept and Example

Principles of a sanctified life and ministry were instilled by my spiritual Mother Green, based on 50 plus years of evangelistic service. Which included preaching, teaching, hospital ministry and a 24-hour prayer room for the Lord. Fortunately, she taught me, counseled, provided shut-ins and weekly all night prayer sessions. Mother Green and her prayer warriors facilitated routine sessions of tarrying for the filling of the Holy Ghost with the evidence of speaking in tongues according to Acts 1:8 KJV

[8] But ye shall receive power, after that the Holy Ghost is come upon you: and ye shall be witnesses unto me both in Jerusalem, and in all Judaea, and in Samaria, and unto the uttermost part of the earth.

Numerous converts were delivered.

During the season, numerous believers were taught biblical principles of salvation, prayers, sanctification and lives were transformed.

North Wells Gospel Mission was founded by the Full Gospel Men's Ministry 501 N. Wells, Chicago, Illinois.

This small church was Pastored by Gaines Alvin Phelp and wife Inez, previously established a mission of temporary dwellings for new converts to Jesus providing a Safe Haven for living, nurturing and teaching of the Word of God.

New converts were supported, empowered and equipped with spiritual and natural skills such as employment training. Having the support necessary for growth and stability as a disciple of Christ, they returned to society. North Wells Gospel Mission was blessed by the Lord to produce many ministries, missionaries and strong Christians North Wells Gospel Mission moved to ---1241 W, 79st Street then to Pastor Martha Graffrey, Pastor Anna Stinson. Currently Bishop George Deal Jr. is pastor. North Wells Temple of Deliverance 2739 W. Madison Ave, Chicago, IL. I was ordained as an evangelist

Jesus ministry began; Jesus sent his disciples out in groups of two, thus I began bedside ministry with Evangelist Sereta Deal, formally my Sunday school student and born again member of North Wells Gospel Mission.

For many years we ministered regularly after work on Mondays. The administration trained us to visit with a population of patients that had no visitors or few family contacts.

The personal Evangelistic Ministry there proved to be fruitful, souls accepted the Lord Jesus, literature was distributed and back sliders were restored. This Evangelistic endeavor increased our strength, faith and determination to serve the Lord Jesus Christ.

The Ministry of Twelve

Mark 6:7-8 KJV then Jesus called the Twelve to him and began to send them out two by two, giving them authority over unclean spirits.

Mark verse 8 He instructed them to take nothing, but a staff for the journey: no bread, no bag, no money in their belts.

The Evangelistic ministry continued as the Holy Spirit led and directed us to various individuals, members of the church, prisons, homes and hospitals.

Evangelism at Cook County Hospital:

Evangelistic training and ministry began in 1980 under the auspices of Chaplain Pembrook, we became members of the Light Bearers Association. Chaplain Pembrook was an anointed, experienced man of God. He taught and demonstrated the Christian application of leading souls to Christ at a critical stage of life. Catastrophe, illness and trauma brings mankind face to face with mortality and eternity. The essential question of life's focus is "What Shall I Do With Jesus?" We ministered the plan of salvation according to Romans Road chapter 10; in this environment evangelistic efforts and results became fruitful and fast. The Holy Spirit moved on consistently, reclaimed, healed and delivered many souls.

Meeting God in The Broken Places

Jesus Ministry Catherine Scott Pastor Memory Deal and his wife Deborah Deal, former Sunday school member, trained at Cook County Hospital with Chaplain Pembrook and joined the Evangelistic team. The Lord opened an effective door of opportunity at Kenwood Nursing Home February 2004.

On Valentine's Day, February 14th, upon entering the program director's office she greeted me "Dr. Boatwright, we have been waiting for you Arthur referred you." Arthur was a volunteer completing required service learning hours. Arthur was a senior in our program at Hyde Park Academy, Chicago, IL.

Developing Jesus Ministry : God's Grace is sufficient to complete life assignments.

Matthew 4:18-19 KJV "and Jesus walking by the Sea of Galilee saw 2 brothers called Peter and Andrew, his brother casting a net into the sea, for they were fishers. And he saith unto them follow me, and I will make you fishers of men."

During this time period of emptiness, failure, confusion and pain, Jesus drew me unto himself. Jesus spoke these words "I am come that you might have life." The Lord baptized me in the precious Holy Ghost on Thursday, September 17, 1971. It happened about 6 o'clock in the home of a sister that I met at Monument of Faith Evangelistic Church. After fasting and staying home from work, one day Jesus baptized me in the Holy Ghost with evidence of speaking in tongues! Totally engulfed in the spirit for hours, I experienced transition to a place of Super Natural Peace! Never desired to return or go Back!

2 Corinthians 5:17 KJV

[17] Therefore if any man be in Christ, he is a new creature: old things are passed away; behold, all things are become new.

This supernatural peace continued to shadow me for days as I returned to my normal life. My life involved teaching school, attending church and bible classes at Monument of Faith and Prayer Meeting with my Godmother!

Scripture; "There is no temptation taken you, but such that as is common to man God will also make a way of escape. A New Born Again Christian must be willing to forsake sin and surrender a life unto God!" Romans 12:1 KJV

"I beseech you therefore brethren by the mercies of God that you present your bodies as a living sacrifice-holy and acceptable unto God, which is your reasonable service. Romans 12:2 KJV and be not conformed to this world but be transformed by the renewing of your mind."

God's Divine Purpose for My Plan

Jesus reveals his immediate plan which was Life, Salvation, and Deliverance!

A Transformation. The Transformed Life When one encounters Jesus, that experience produces a dramatic, internal and external change.

Visible change occurs that others can see. Acts 4:13 KJV "Now when they saw the boldness, and perceived that they were unlearned and ignorant men, they marveled, and they took knowledge of them that they had been with Jesus."

When a touch from Jesus caused the scales to fall from our spiritual eyes and ears, supernatural empowerment was given by the falling of the Holy Ghost. The Holy Spirit gives the believer boldness, courage, confidence, and wisdom that is supernatural. This empowers one to live a faith filled, spirit-filled life disciplined life of holiness and obedience to the word of God. Jesus revealed himself to me as the Holy Spirit drew me, I lost the joy of the activities that I was enjoying. The Holy Spirit began to give dreams and revelations and convictions of sin in my life!

On a Friday evening in this season, I dressed for a party that I had been invited to. Having no desire to attend, I sat at my kitchen table with a quart of Budweiser and my bible, having decided not to attend. The Lord Jesus spoke to me in an audible voice, Jesus spoke these words, "I am come that you might have life", when he spoke to me, I knew who He was. What a mystery, it blessed my soul and the disciples recorded the same experience in John 21:12 KJV "Jesus saith unto them come and dine" and further confirmed to me that Jesus is real. Jesus speaks to us through His word, through dreams and vision! The Lord also speaks to us in a clear method that is individualized for that person,

The Lord Jesus is the Good Shepherd who knows how to reveal himself to each sheep. God the Holy Spirit will teach us how to develop a relationship with Him as John 1:13-14 KJV and 16:13-14 KJV. We obey the word and surrender our lives.

A Journey of Faith, Establishment of Jesus Ministries

Hebrews 12:6 KJV "But without faith, it is impossible to please him: For he that cometh to God must believe that he is a rewarder of them that diligently seek him."

Each and every born again Christian has been called to implement the Great Commission in Matthew 28:18-20: "And Jesus came and spoke unto the, saying all power is given unto me in heaven and in earth; 19 Go ye therefore and teach all nations, baptizing them in the name of the Father, and of the Son and of the Holy Ghost;20 Teaching them to observe all things whatsoever I have commanded you; and lo, I am with you always, even unto the end of the world."

In obedience to this command and teaching, I began to minister at Warren Barr Nursing Home on Dearborn in Chicago, Illinois. Best practice principles of bedside ministry and strategies training received at Moody Bible Institute, pragmatic, cultural application to observe that Arthur exceeds required hours, at the nursing home (Arthur has performed over 300 hours). Arthur shared his enthusiasm and love for the clients and staff. The Lord used his experience to motivate and lead me and the team to begin our ministry at Kenwood Nursing Home Hyde Park, Illinois.

There was no formal name for the team, however, it was required for application. Prayerfully, seeking the Lord for a name he spoke: "Jesus Ministries" scripture Matthew 4:19 "and he saith unto them, follow me, and I will make you fishers of men." Thank the Lord, as we follow Jesus he teaches us how to be fishers of men. Jesus went about preaching repentance, and the good news of the kingdom of heaven. We must do the same for the people who sat in darkness and have seen the great light Jesus Ministry began at this facility on the first Saturday of each month. The team consisted of Pastor Deal and Evangelist Deal and myself. We were privileged to ministry to five residents at that time.

The ministry has grown consistently into the current population of 45-60 residents. The first Saturday of each month, the ministry disciples' souls, discipling includes creative bible tutoring activities, guest ministers, social service groups such as Boy Scouts and parents. God's eyes are upon the faithful of the land. The Bible teaches us not to despise small beginnings. The Lord has demonstrated both his anointing and faithful plan and purpose for Jesus Ministry.

A Season of Deliverance and Salvation Transformation

A season of supernatural grace, a Holy Ghost movement like a Mighty wind the Holy Ghost began to move, among our congregation. According to (Acts 2:1-4; 2:1KJV) And when the day of Pentecost was fully come, they were all with one accord in one place. Acts 2:2 KJV. And suddenly there came a sound from heaven as of a rushing mighty wind, and it filled all the house where they were sitting. Acts 2:3 KJV And there appeared unto them cloven tongues like as of fire, and it sat upon each of them. 2:4 And they were all filled with the Holy Ghost as the spirit gave utterance.

A spiritual awakening occurred in the church kingdom (world) during the period of 1989-1991. Spiritual growth and seeking the Lord was highly demonstrated at North Wells Gospel Mission. A weekly prayer meeting was organized, and met every Thursday night in the basement of Deacon George Deal Sr. This home represented the moral and spiritual lighthouse of that community, at N. Clybourn Street Chicago, Illinois.

An African American community of migrants from the south, they had settled here seeking economic advancement. Rich in a fundamental knowledge of the bible and a love for the Lord and the church, Deacon Deal Sr. was highly respected as the Father of the community. Also, a greatly loved and faithful Deacon for our church.

The members of his family, members of the church and seekers needing prayer assembled weekly. The Lord anointed me as the primary teacher, leader and facilitator to teach about the gifts of the Holy Spirit. The promise and need for the second gift of grace was taught during this period. A revelation of Hell and Heaven was revealed in a book. Mary Kay Baxter wrote "30 Days in Hell", a vivid description of her experience.

The Depths of Hell

Like a supernatural-A Movement of the Holy Ghost: Many lives were/have been forever transformed by the powerful blood of Jesus and the word of God. It was very motivating, informative and inspiring, the seekers were healed, delivered and filled with the Holy Ghost.

In a Supernatural Journey!

1976 In a divine revelation of Hell over a period of 30 nights, God gave Mary K Baxter visions of hell and commissioned her to tell people still alive on earth to reject sin and evil, and to choose life in Christ.

This literature combined with the word motivated, inspired and softened the hearts of the participants. Employing the spiritual keys of faith, prayer, persistence and love into the ministry built the foundation for Jesus Christ to manifest Supernatural Power.

The greatest struggle of my life has been submitting, living, yielding and obeying the Lord's perfect will as a single woman. This experience reflects the greatest victory in my life, teaching me the reality of 1 Corinthians 12:9…"and He said unto me my grace is sufficient for thee: for my strength is made perfect in weakness."

The greatest challenge of my life: Becoming the caretaker for my Godmother and assuming management of her affairs for 4 years. This was daunting, because I functioned as a Chicago Public School administrator pursuing a Doctorate at Roosevelt and teaching Sunday School simultaneously. This experience reflects my greatest victory when the Apostle Paul wrote "I can do all things through Christ."

My greatest victory has been witnessing the Lord deliver each of my siblings saved and filled them with the Holy Spirit.

Procrastination is my greatest issue regretfully, | didn't surrender my life to the Lord earlier. Gladys Knight expresses my story best in song (paraphrasing) "If anyone should ever write my life story, tell them Jesus is the Best Thing That Ever Happened To Me!!

A Season of World Pandemics

The contemporary journey of life encompasses a World Pandemic of the Covid-19 virus. The church still has God's grace available today, the power of wisdom, peace and victory is in Jesus Christ. Apostle Paul wrote to the Hebrews, facing challenges and struggles with the eternal promise of God's Word.

Hebrews 13:8 KJV Jesus Christ the same yesterday, today and forever.

The journey of life is filled with swift transitions, there is nothing, new "under the Sun" (scripture)

Dr. David Jerimiah declared on May 8, 2020 on the National Day of Prayer the Lord revealed the true World's Pandemic is SIN! Covid-19 is employed to shift mankind to brokenness, humility, repentance, revival, restoration and healing. As the country grapples naturally and spiritually with the World's Pandemic, Jesus Christ remains the same.

Dr. G. Yvette Boatwright

As a Life-long Educator for more than thirty years, I functioned as a Special Education teacher, Resource Teacher, Administrative Facilitator of a high school, Assistant Principal of two elementary Chicago Public schools, Adjunct Professor of Education at Concordia University, Sunday School & Bible Teacher & a committed Lifelong learner. My Philosophy is a commitment to lifelong learning and a belief that education provides a rite of passage to life in society. A Belief that everyone has a right to the privilege of education and development of their various skills in America.

Jesus Ministry

Season of Pandemic

Contemporary Heroes of Faith in the Pandemic World of 2020

The church of Jesus Christ in a pandemic world champion and embrace the word of God the Bible is a firm foundation in these problematic times. Jesus Christ does not change!

Matthew 16:18 KJV " and I say unto thee thou are Peter and upon this rock, I will build my church and the gates of Hell shall not prevail against it."

The year 2020 has been a watershed moment at a time of awakening, conflict and crisis in America, a time of revealing, social injustice, social and economic disparity, discrimination, depression and despair.

The World of Medical Pandemic revealed and presented an opportunity for God's plan and purpose in a contemporary world. The Sin Pandemic which closed the physical church. A time of social injustice, political insurrection, an unprecedented presidential election has shocked and humbled America. This moment has inspired, ignited and called us to our God! Contemporary Heroes of Faith champion the principles of faith in God and righteousness in every aspect and area of life.

The Secular World

God revealed a contemporary hero of faith in the life of Chadwick Boseman the Black Panther. He is a testimony of faith, grace, and strength living with cancer serving others, visiting sick children, while working to finish his work on earth. A 43 yr old bearing his cancer humbly without complaint. A testimony that God increases faith, grace and strength when we obey and trust Jesus and the Word of God.

Our world has changed drastically over a few months yet God has not changed. A season of health crisis, social injustice and moral decline, and death. God wants us to stand strong in our faith. When you look at the wind and waves, you start to sink, but when you fix your eyes on Jesus you start to rise and you can walk on water. For he has promised us, "with God all things are possible". (Matthew 19-26 KJV)

Where do we get that faith? It's simple: looking unto Jesus the author and finisher of our faith. (Hebrews 12:2 KJV - Looking unto Jesus the author and finisher of our faith;)

When we hold onto him we can overcome any obstacle, Mr. Gordon Robertson presents the testimony of God's power, provision and presences for CBN Asia in the Philippines. For 7 months, there was never enough money for payroll, gathered to pray, and each time God would do a miracle, providing the money within 24 hours.

Today God has given a great commission to Christian Ambassadors to preach the Gospel. COV-19 season provides a supernatural opportunity to humble mankind and prepare hearts to receive the Gospel of Jesus Christ.

Gordon Robertson is President and Chief Executive Officer of CBN and Founder of CBN Asia.,Jne and Center for Missions excerpted from an on live CBN Staff Chapel teaching, scripture is quoted from the NKJV.

History fuels our present and guides future experiences. Past events represent and confirm that God is faithful, yesterday, today, and forever. Heroes of faith are approaching the ministry with new church ministry strategies during COVID-19.

A season of transformation, turmoil and transition.

Ecclesiastes 3:1 KJV "to everything there is a season and a time to every purpose under heaven." Our world has changed dramatically over the past few months - yet God has not changed and he wants us to stand strong in our faith.

The Lord is blessing Us Today Heroes of Faith in Jesus Christ speak to these circumstances with the Holy Spirit's spiritual gifts.

God manifests power and presence today April 25, 2022, the Lord gave me a vision. Vision of the robbery of my home the word "faith" was written on the wall in bold white letters.

Robbery of my home furniture, everything pillows from church were in the living room. The entire house was empty. My friend Faye Caldwell was present. Looking around in shock! "I stated I have been robbed". Then I heard the scripture John 10:10 loud and clear. "The thief cometh not, but for to steal, and to kill, and to destroy: I am come that they might have life, and that they might have it more abundantly."

I awoke suddenly and realized that this had been a vision! Holy Spirit the Lord's to reveal that faith in the Lord will empower and sustain Christians during this season.

Faith: Now faith is the substance (title deed of things hoped for the evidence of things not seen. For by it the elders obtained a good report Hebrews 11:12 KJV

God's heroes of Faith demonstrate an active, unwavering faith in Jesus Christ and the Word of God.

Today it is significant for the older group to teach and remember God's power of deliverance Egypt by crossing the Red Sea. Today the miracle for the younger generation is to navigate life by God's power. Lives of these Heroes of Faith exemplify that God's people can place faith in the promises of God. When God speaks he is able to guide into the promised land. God, the Holy Spirit leads, comforts, provides and overcomes all obstacles.

When God speaks, one is challenged to trust, surrender, obey and walk by faith into the Promised Land.

II Corinthians 5:7 (For we walk by faith, not by sight) God's Heroes Of Faith in our contemporary world dramatically changing times champion steadfast, incredible astounding faith in the Bible.

God's Heroes of Faith demonstrate belief in spiritual visions, dreams, signs and prophecy!

Amos 3:7 KJV Surely the lord God will do nothing but he revealeth his secret unto his servants the prophets.

Conclusion

Keys to God's Presence and Power Walking with God Today:

First, just as Enoch did, we are to walk by faith. 2 Corinthians 5:7 says we are to walk by faith and not by sight.

Second, our walk with God is a walk in the spirit. Roman 8:1 tells us to "walk not after the flesh, but after the Spirit."

Third, we are to walk in the light of God's word. We are to feed upon the word of God daily and walk in the truth.

Fourth, we walk in fellowship with God and one another. The Blood of Jesus cleanses us from all sin so one can walk in fellowship with God and fellow Christians (I John 1:3,7 KJV)

When we get to the end of our lives, people should be able to say that we walked with God. The time is short, and the day is fast approaching when Jesus will return to the earth. Today more than ever, we need to learn how to walk with God (Editor's note: This Article was adapted from Kenneth E. Hagin's book Classic Sermons.)

Hebrews 13:8 KJV Jesus Christ the same yesterday and today and forever.

The church still has God's Grace available today.

Power, Wisdom, and Grace

1. We serve and retain an unchanging Christ in changing times.
2. Jesus Christ never changes.
3. We live in a dying world that is constantly changing.
4. Jesus is giving Grace and Power today.

God's Heroes of faith in contemporary times champion the identical meaning of the memorial stones from the Jordan River.

Joshua 4:6-8 KJV and Joshua set twelve stones in the midst of Jordan, at the spot where the priest who carried the ark of the covenant had stood; and they are there to this day.

The importance of the stones remains constant today- Serves as a focus for us to remember the miracles that God performed to deliver the Hero elites.

Supernatural Empowerment: Acts 4:33 KJV and with great power gave the apostles witness of the resurrection of the Lord Jesus great grace was upon them all.

Abraham believed God's promise that he would have a of his own genealogy (Genesis 15:4 KJV) Descendants were important especially Sons. Abraham was 75 when he first received God's promise, and the promise was not fulfilled until he was 100! The Father of Faith and contemporary heroes of faith have championed these principles of Christians walking with God throughout all seasons.

- Disregard the age bracket
- Disregard the economy and stock market
- Disregard circumstances
- Disregard the voices around you
- Disregard cultural, and racial biases

Faith in God's word and circumstances provides. "Standing ground" is a firm foundation as we navigate our journey. Jesus is the Way, He is able. Abraham believed God to perform every word of his good promises!

God's Contemporary Heroes of Faith demonstrates the evidence of a supernatural God who intervenes and works in the lives of people according to the Bible. Now the Lord had said unto Abram, Get thee out of thy country, and from thy kindred, and from thy father's house, unto a land that I will shew thee:

2 And I will make of thee a great nation, and I will bless thee, and make thy name great; and thou shalt be a blessing: he staggered not at the promise of God through unbelief: but was strong in faith: giving glory to God and being fully persuaded that what he had promised, he was also able to perform.

Supernatural is that which is miraculous and transcends the laws of nature. Supernatural means over and above what is considered natural or normal. Supernatural outcomes are evident in the ministry outcomes over and above what is considered natural or normal.

In the Old Testament, Moses represents the Law and Elijah the prophets. James 5:17 (ESV) says, "Elijah was a man with a nature like ours." To Jewish believers, Elijah was the greatest prophet. Yet James said he was just like you and me.

Heroes of Faith walked in agreement with God. Amos 3:3 KJV says "can two walk together, except they agreed?" To walk with God today requires agreement with his word, purpose and plans. God reveals his power, plans and purpose for an assignment. We should endeavor to stay in step with God, obeying his will and moving in his timing.

Bibliography

King, Martin Luther, Jr. *Strength to Love*. Philadelphia: Fortress Press, 1963.

Mitchell, Henry H. Black *Preaching: The Recovery of a Powerful Art*. Nashville: Abingdon Press, 1990.

Eubanks, Steve. *Quotable King*. Nashville, TN: TowleHouse Publishing, 2002.

Brown, Judie. *It Is I Who Have Chosen You*. American Life League, 1997.

The Living Bible Paraphrased. Wheaton, Illinois: Tyndale House Publishers, 1971.

Loritts, Bryan, ed. Letters to a Birmingham Jail: A Response to the Words and Dreams of Dr. *Martin Luther King, Jr.* Chicago: Moody Publishers, 2014.

Jakes, T.D. *Maximize the Moment: Gods Action Plan for Your Life*. G.P. Putnam and Sons, 1999.

Jeremiah, David, Dr. *The Lord Reveals the Two World Pandemics*. Magazine, v. XXX, Date.

NIV Life Applications Study Bible. Grand Rapids, Michigan: Zondervan and Carols Stream, Illinois :Tyndale House Publishers, Inc, 2011.

The American Roget's College Thesaurus in Dictionary Form: Rev ed. New York: New American Library, 1978.

How to Write & Sell Your First Novel. Cincinnati, Ohio: Writer's Digest Book, 1997.

We Can Walk With God, Timeless Teachings of Kenneth E. Hagin

Printed in the United States
by Baker & Taylor Publisher Services